Masterpiece Mix

ROXIE MUNRO

HOLIDAY HOUSE · NEW YORK

TODAY I will make a new painting.

First I build the stretcher.

Then I stretch
the canvas

and put gesso, a white
coating, on it.

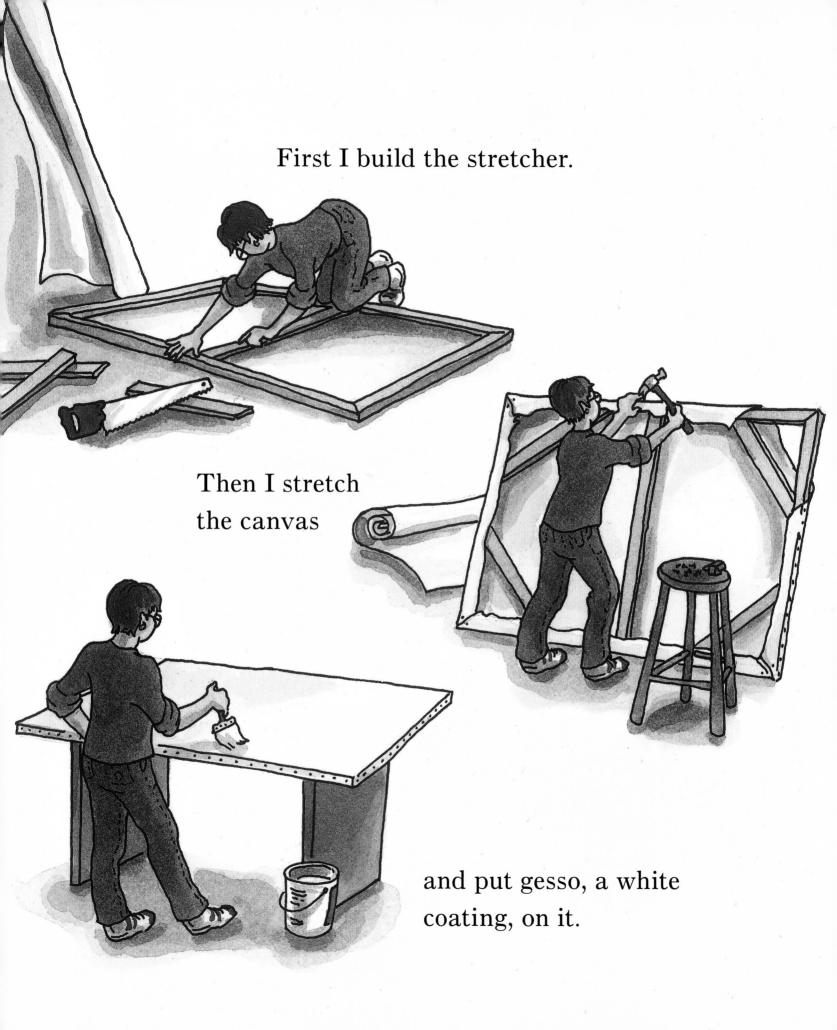

I get out all my tools: tubes of oil paint,

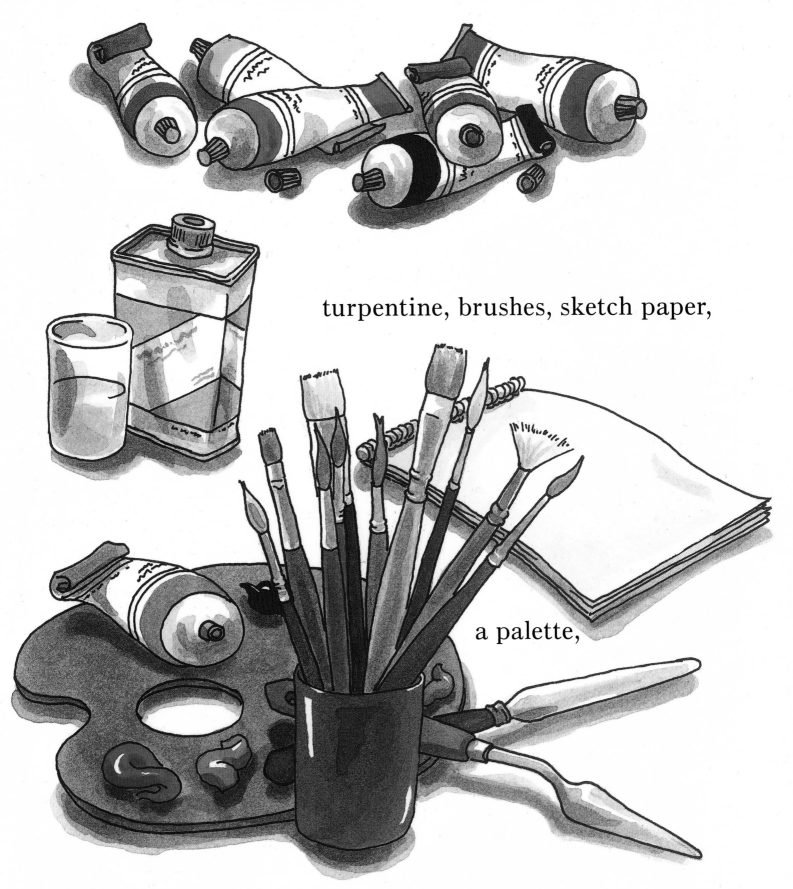

turpentine, brushes, sketch paper,

a palette,

and palette knives for mixing colors.

But what should I paint?

I study great still life
paintings from the museum.

A still life has objects in it
that do not move.

Landscapes are
popular.
Landscapes show places.

Many artists
do portraits.

Portraits are pictures of
people . . .

or animals!

Figure studies are important.
They show the human body.

Many artists like cultural
subjects, such as dance,
music, art, and literature . . .

or even sports!

My father always said,
"Do what you really love."

KEY TO THE ART IN THIS BOOK

1 Robert S. Duncanson was the rare African American painter whose work was preserved before the 20th century. He loved painting portraits and landscapes and was influenced by the Hudson River School. *Still Life with Fruit and Nuts* was painted in oil on board in 1848.

2 *Jerusalem Artichoke Flowers* (oil on canvas) was made in 1880 by the French Impressionist Claude Monet. He was fascinated by nature and changing light and painted haystacks, the Rouen Cathedral, and water-lily ponds dozens of times in different seasons and many light conditions.

3 Frenchman Paul Cézanne painted *Still Life with Apples and Peaches* in oil in 1905. He's sometimes called the Father of Cubism and is known for building forms with planes and color and for not using traditional perspective.

4 As is true of many artists, Cézanne's family discouraged him from becoming a painter, but he is now one of the most renowned artists in the world. The small oil painting *Three Pears*, made in 1879, is typical of many of his still life paintings.

5 Vincent van Gogh is one of my favorite artists. He worked fast, with a distinctive brushstroke, using vivid colors and patterns. He was Dutch but painted mainly in Paris and the south of France. The oil painting *Roses* was made in 1890 a few weeks before he died at the age of thirty-seven.

6 Winslow Homer mainly painted life in America, where he traveled widely in the late 19th century. This painting, though, is a watercolor called *Salt Kettle, Bermuda*. He also created oil paintings, and early in his career illustrated thirteen children's books.

7 The English artist John Constable was acclaimed for his landscapes and his clouds. After studying classic landscape masters such as Titian and Claude Lorrain he started painting directly from nature. This is one of his oil paintings, *Wivenhoe Park, Essex*, made in 1816.

8 *Flower Beds in Holland* is an early oil on canvas and wood painted by Vincent van Gogh in 1883. Although van Gogh made more than 900 paintings in his life, he only sold one while he was alive. He is now one of the most famous artists ever.

9 Claude Monet painted *The Japanese Footbridge* in oil in 1899. He created beautiful gardens at his home in Giverny, France, and was fascinated by light reflecting on water. He did more than 250 paintings of just the water-lily pond, keeping it clean and dusting it so reflections appeared clearly on its surface.

 **10** Frédéric Bazille was going to be a doctor, but he really wanted to paint. He studied with the Impressionists and created *Young Woman with Peonies* (oil on canvas) in 1870. He died young, at the age of twenty-eight, fighting in the Franco-Prussian War.

 **11** Like many artists, Paul Gauguin did self-portraits. This one from 1889 is oil painted on wood. Gauguin worked for years as a Paris stockbroker, but he preferred to be an artist. He painted in Paris, southern France (where he lived with van Gogh), and Tahiti. He spent his last years in the Marquesas Islands.

 **12** Van Gogh painted at least forty-three self-portraits. Several show his bandaged right ear, which he cut partially off in a fit of depression. This vivid *Self-Portrait* (oil on canvas) was created in Arles in the south of France in 1889.

 13 American portrait painter Gilbert Stuart did many paintings of the Father of Our Country, George Washington. He did portraits of four other presidents as well and of many society people of his time. This oil on canvas was painted between 1803 and 1805.

 **14** Mary Cassatt was born in America but went to France at age twenty-two. She lived in Paris most of her life where she became friends with, and was influenced by, the Impressionists. This work in pastel, *The Black Hat*, was made in 1890.

 **15** Johannes Vermeer, a Dutch artist, was fascinated with the effects of light. In this small oil on a panel done in the mid-1660s, *Girl with the Red Hat*, you can see the way he used contrasting darks and lights as well as dramatic highlights on the face and fabric.

 16 Very independent, Mary Cassatt never married. She had no children, but she loved to paint them. In 1886, she created this oil painted on canvas called *Child in Straw Hat*. The little girl looks like she is tired of modeling!

17   Light is important in *Girl with a Flute*, a small oil painted on a panel and attributed to Vermeer. It is believed to have been painted between 1665 and 1675. He worked very slowly and didn't make many paintings. He died at age forty-three and left a wife and eleven children without much money. Now he is considered one of the greatest painters of the Dutch Golden Age.

18   Also Dutch, portrait painter Frans Hals was admired for his colorful palette and bold brushwork. He painted wealthy or prominent patrons in Holland, including, in the 1630s, this *Portrait of a Member of the Haarlem Civic Guard*, which was painted in oil on canvas.

19   British artist George Stubbs was well known for his animal paintings, especially his carefully studied dogs and horses. He even published a book called *The Anatomy of the Horse*. Stubbs did this big oil painting, *White Poodle in a Punt*, in 1780.

20   The French painter Edgar Degas also studied the anatomy, musculature, and movement of horses, including racehorses in action. Here, though, in this small oil painting on canvas, *Horses in a Meadow*, done in 1871, they are resting.

21   Henri Rousseau worked for years as a customs inspector in Paris before becoming a full-time self-taught artist. Rousseau never left France, but he created imaginative landscapes using patterns and flat colors, as you can see in one of his last paintings, *Tropical Forest with Monkeys*. He created it in 1910.

22   Although Frenchman Édouard Manet usually painted modern life in mid-19th-century Paris, he also did work like this oil painted on linen, using bold brushwork and called *A King Charles Spaniel*, done in 1866.

23   The great Flemish painter Peter Paul Rubens was a scholar, a diplomat, and spoke seven languages. To make this huge oil painting, *Daniel in the Lions' Den* (almost 9 by 12½ feet!), Rubens carefully studied and drew the lions in the royal menagerie in Brussels and at the Ghent Zoo. It is believed to have been painted between 1614 and 1616.

24 Philadelphia-born James McNeill Whistler studied art in Paris and worked in London most of his life. He was celebrated mainly for his portraits. This print, *Walter Sickert*, was done in 1895 and is of a well-known German artist friend.

25 Although Paul Gauguin's work in oil became more colorful and abstract after he moved to French Polynesia, he continued to do figure studies, like *Tahitians Gathering Fruit*, a delicate drawing in graphite and blue pencil on paper (1899–1900).

26 Cassatt studied art at the Pennsylvania Academy of Fine Arts. Because she was a woman, she wasn't allowed to take life drawing classes. But she wanted to be an artist, against her parents' wishes, and moved to Paris for the rest of her life. *The Caress* was made in 1891.

27 The great Dutch artist Rembrandt worked in the 17th century. He was known for his use of dramatic light. You can see the strong contrast between dark and light in this small brush and brown wash drawing called *Beggar Woman Leaning on a Stick*.

28 Frenchman Honoré Daumier created thousands of paintings, prints, sculptures, and drawings in the 19th century, such as *The Young Courier* (crayon and wash on paper). Scholars don't know when he drew it. He did lots of political caricatures. One even landed him in jail! Toward the end of his life, sadly, the great draftsman became blind.

29 This large oil painting by American James McNeill Whistler, which is seven feet high, is called *The White Girl*. It is from 1862. It was rejected from several major art exhibitions in Europe but is now one of his most famous paintings.

30 Besides painting racehorses Degas loved dance and made more than 1,000 drawings, paintings, and sculptures on ballet. He worked for several years on this sculpture, called *Little Dancer Aged Fourteen* (1878–1881). The original, made from wax, had satin slippers, a muslin tutu, and a wig of human hair.

31   American William Michael Harnett painted *The Old Violin* in oil on canvas in 1886. It is an example of trompe l'oeil, which means fool the eye. When it was first exhibited, a guard was posted in the gallery to make sure people didn't try to touch it.

32   Dutch artist Judith Leyster achieved success unusual for a woman in the early 17th century. She was a member of the artists' guild and had several students. This oil painting is a self-portrait, showing a laughing Leyster painting in her studio in 1630.

33   Jean-Honoré Fragonard, a Frenchman, was a master of the pastoral landscape and the domestic scene. He used lush brushwork and created poetic atmospheres. This oil on canvas called *Young Girl Reading* was painted in 1770, during an artistic period called rococo.

34   Another of my favorite artists is Edward Hopper, a 20th-century American painter. Better known for his moody interiors and evocative New York City scenes, he also painted rural subjects. Hopper spent summers on Cape Cod, where he was inspired to create this oil painting, *Ground Swell*, in 1939.

35   Winslow Homer made several versions of this oil painting, *Breezing Up (A Fair Wind)*, from 1873 to 1876. He did oil paintings and watercolors of rural life, usually sportsmen hunting or fishing, and outdoor scenes of people at work or play. We kept a print of this painting on the dining room wall of my childhood home.

36   George Bellows was a member of the Ashcan School—a group of New York City artists who painted city scenes, neighborhoods, street life, and boxing and other sports in the early 1900s. One of his most famous oils is *Both Members of This Club*, painted in 1909.

37   A Philadelphian, portrait painter Thomas Eakins had a lifelong interest in the human figure. He studied anatomy and worked with photography. His style was considered realism. He painted many subjects, including boxers, swimmers, and, in oil in 1872, these rowers, *The Biglin Brothers Racing*.

*

To my dear longtime friends and art collectors extraordinaire,
Susan Vallon and Andy Beyer of Washington, DC

*

ACKNOWLEDGMENTS

All art images courtesy of the National Gallery of Art in Washington, DC. The paintings shown
in this book were obtained through the NGA's Open Access policy, which has digitalized images of more
than 45,000 works of art available in the public domain (usually created prior to the 1920s). Special thanks
to Heidi Hinish, the Head of Gallery and Studio Learning at the National Gallery of Art.

National Gallery of Art:
http://www.nga.gov/content/ngaweb.html

NGA Open Access:
https://images.nga.gov/en/page/show_home_page.html

*

HOLIDAY HOUSE is registered in the U.S. Patent and Trademark Office.
Printed and bound in April 2017 at Toppan Leefung, DongGuan City, China.
The artwork was created in mixed media with India ink and colored acrylic inks on paper, and collage using giclee prints.
www.holidayhouse.com
First Edition
1 3 5 7 9 10 8 6 4 2
Library of Congress Cataloging-in-Publication Data

Names: Munro, Roxie, author, illustrator.
Title: Masterpiece mix / Roxie Munro.
Description: First edition. | New York : Holiday House, 2017. | Audience:
Ages 4–8. | Audience: K to grade 3.
Identifiers: LCCN 2016048118 | ISBN 9780823436996 (hardcover)
Subjects: LCSH: Painting—Themes, motives—Juvenile literature. | Art
Genres—Juvenile literature. | National Gallery of Art (U.S.)—Juvenile literature.
Classification: LCC ND1288.M86 2017 | DDC 751—dc23 LC record available at
https://lccn.loc.gov/2016048118